b

nds & Letters 7

KNOWLEDGE BOOKS

bed	ball
bat	box
bag	bug
boy	

bed

3

ball

5

bat

box

9

bag

11

bug

boy

15

bed	ball
bat	box
bag	bug
boy	

Knowledge Books and Software
PO Box 50 Sandgate, Queensland 4017 Australia
p. +617-55680288 f. +617-55680277 email: sales@kbs.com.au

First Published 2022
ISBN 9781922516794
Text and editing: Carole Crimeen
Design and layout: Suzanne Fletcher
Publisher: Robert Watts

Series Information: **Sounds and Letters**

Credits
Photographs: Cover © wee dezign; p. 1 © Daria Rybakova, MaraZe, Kindlena, Africa Studio; p.
3 © Dima Moroz; p. 5 © Stepan Bormotov; p. 7 © Sanit Fuangnakhon; p. 9 © Africa Studio; p.
11 © JIANG HONGYAN; p. 13 © Alex Staroseltsev; p. 15 © Africa Studio/Shutterstock.

Phonic support books are a wonderful resource for emergent readers as they encourage independent reading and help students make the link between letters and the sounds they represent.

Have students identify the images on the title page to listen for the sound that they will hear through the book.

Encourage students to point to each word as they read through the book.

ISBN: 9781922516794

9 781922 516794 >

KNOWLEDGE BOOKS

Sounds&
Letters